AF413828

50
Golden
Pieces

BlueInk
SCRIBBLE

50 Golden Pieces

JEAN RENÉ BAZIN PIERREPIERRE

Table of Contents

Preamble

Our Father

Once upon an afternoon, in my neighborhood, I watched a car park.
Out came a man, sleeves half way up, tie loosened from a day's work.
He came around the car to the rear passenger door and helped out a
young child still peppy from her daycare. While keeping an eye on her,
he gathered books and briefcase,
then picked her up on the way to the front door. She insisted on
carrying something for her dad. "Daddy, let me help you", she went on
till he gave in and gave her the lightest book.
She proudly grabbed it against her little chest. She was so happy that
she went on kissing Daddy's face so repeatedly.
They made their way to the house; he smiling at her, she kissing his face
and still hugging the book.
But what her little toddler years did not grasp is that if she could
kiss Daddy's face while holding the book, making it to the house, it's
because Daddy was carrying her and the book…

We can decide to kiss Daddy's face or just throw a tantrum or a fit;
we will still be in the arms of Our Father, carrying us with our load…
leading us safely home.

Foreword

HE who can put a halt
To mighty waves' madness,
Knows as well how to thwart
The devil's wickedness.

To E.N.

When in this life turmoil
We let go of our hands,
The souls in sorrow toil
But in embrace remain...

Then comes under the light
The bleeding of our hearts
All crushed under this plight
Since their world's torn apart.

The Lotto

Softly cuddling
With his old fling
The poor man thinks of lotto.
He makes his plans
When hunger pangs
Deep in his stomach, echo.

And in the dark
Where no dogs bark,
Asleep he dreams of lotto.
With a dollar
Gladly holler,
Change the curse of long ago.

But as he dreams
He hears a scream
Short of buying the lotto.
She felt something
Crawl up her shin
And had to belch her solo.

"Sleep on," he said
Just as he laid
His head back on the pillow
In dire need
To join the feed
And dream playing the lotto.

Divine Dilemma

Within the cold of desert nights,
From the sky fall loads of fires,
Decisive answer of a fight
When the world patience expires,

Within the cold of scary nights,
Children from their fear galvanized
Are closing ears and eyes so tight
Unjustly reproved and chastised.

"Oh! Bin Laden, what have you done?
What did you expect from this one?
Round the globe the City snivels,
Why hate so much the infidels?"

Within the pain of bleeding hearts,
The sorrow runs on dust and steel
And the families torn apart
Will always bear this dreading feel.

Within the hearts of Love divine
His blood is shed the world over
For tomorrow the sun will shine
On all His children wherever.

Easter's Hopes

So here we are again in this time of the year
When all the hopes we have come in to dry our tears.
Hope for a tomorrow that would bring in advance
The little child in us given yet one more chance.

Hope of a better us, a more loving person,
A kind and patient one, a not-so-busy one.
One who would take the time to smell of the flowers
The fragrance of petals in the evening hours.

Hope to grasp with the heart the beauty of all things,
Not to miss their input while making a living.
Hope to give the neighbor what we wish to receive,
Hope that with our quota our world we don't deceive.

But then we realize that the same promises
Were uttered silently as last Easter wishes.
And we meet face to face with the revelation
That many times the thoughts speak louder than actions…

Happy Easter again! It's the wish we send you.
May the love that you give to your thoughts may be true,
And may the Force who made this good day possible
Remain with you always, make you strong and able!

Sun, Earth and Clouds

Do you see o'er the hills rolling blankets of clouds
Spreading fast on the vale just like despairing shrouds,
Reminding all the birds that south should be their way
And robbing of us all of the gentle sunrays?

And morosely the sun kisses the earth goodbye.
There will be days ahead he will see her pass by
Guessing her green contours and her seas of pure jade.
He'll miss watching her roll and in circle parade.

Oh! He has lots of stars to shine his warmth upon
But among them the earth remains the favorite one.
She always entertains his eyes without presage,
Always changing the tone of her lovely visage.

Then he tries desperately the melt the clouds away.
And it rains, and it pours. There spring is on its way.
There will be days ahead he will watch her roll by
But until then the sun missing the earth will sigh.

Hurricane

Is that you emanate from the depths of ocean
Or that from high above you are sent to nations?
It remains that from your power of destruction
You bring about great threat to all population.

You set destination and suddenly take charge.
Woe to whosoever fails to remain at large.
You go forth, powerful, never take any pose,
Not caring for the plans you decide to oppose.

Your eye the terrible center of disaster
Seems to see the secret of any connivance.
It destroys ruthlessly considering never
Whether it's night or day. Nothing can stand a chance.

Of your winds the power nothing on earth resists.
The planes, gigantic trees, buildings, to say the least,
Can barely overcome the destroying effect.
Even human spirits so often you deject

The sea and its waters come join to your fury.
The waves are vigorous, potent, even mighty.
They seem to help battle siding with your madness,
Every living party, making all a big mess.

But tell me do you know how many lives you claim?
Innocent children death for which you are to blame,
Taken while they're sleeping. They were quarries so lame.
Of your waters in rage should you not be ashamed?

Then again tell me who can fathom the reason
So painful experience is forced upon someone?
The lucky ones He spares should always lend a hand
For us all, the good Lord has lots to reprimand.

Fair Exchange

The bull nonchalantly carries
The pack of birds that pick its fleas.
And the birds resting trustingly
Feast and ride away happily.

The tree with its mighty shadow
Allows the water spring to grow
By protecting it from sunshine.
One day a riverbank it'll find.
In return it will silently
Quench to its fill the mighty tree.

The cattle graze on the meadow
From today's dawn till tomorrow
And the next day. But O surprise!
By relieving, they fertilize
The soil that gives the good herbage
That will become their best pottage…

Maybe one day we'll comprehend
The lessons forever at hand…
Truly one can fully mature
Closely watching Mother Nature.

"Keep Hope Alive"

Have faith my loving child! Trust in your tomorrow
And in the days to come! Don't give in your sorrow.
Hope at every sunrise and kneel before the Lord.
Come pray relentlessly for what you can't afford.

Sins, faults and trespasses cause our sufferings.
Maybe after the Lord righteous and forgiving,
Compensates His angels, His saints and all His justs,
Will He mercifully look 'pon us the unjusts.

When the years were still young we failed to comprehend
That what we throw one way comes back the other hand.
And in our failures, those we once called mischiefs,
We never realized we were our own thieves.

Have faith then my sweet child and maybe tomorrow,
Just like He created free eagle, free sparrow,
The Lord will free your soul from all its wickedness.
So hope my loving child, have faith in His goodness.

Exodus I and II

O Lord, from Your heavens, Your divine Paradise,
You have with all your might tried to evangelize
This people of Your choice, not worthy of Your love,
But made by Your strong will citizens of above.

You tried, loving Father, all through their existence,
Faithfully to expose them to the quintessence
Of Your creation and the real meaning of life.
You sent many prophets to lead them on the path.

Moses was a great one chosen within Pharaoh's
Taken right from the midst of all Ramses' arrows.
He showed them many times of Your arm the power,
Separating the sea, firing down Your anger.

But in their stubbornness and their coldness of hearts
They always drift astray and from Your love depart.
But You, their Creator, rich in divine mercy
Planned the ultimate scheme for their safe re-entry.

For they can re-enter keeping eyes on Your Christ,
Your perfect offering, the lamb divinely priced.
They will return safely to Your gracious heavens
Solely based on their faith all at Your Son's expense

Dear Father, make them see, we beseech You today,
Your efforts and Your works designed to make them pray
To You, divine Source of everlasting richness,
To You, the beginning, the end and nothing less.

What a Beautiful World

The world is so full of beauty,
So heart-throbbing in ecstasy,
That a lifetime would not suffice
To see it all at any price.

On any given blessed day,
The sun with the warmth of its rays
Ignites a spark of loneliness
That daily flows from Heavens' nest.

But if for some lazy reason
From this dazzling scene you'd seen none,
Birds with grateful tunes will convey
To your sleepy ears, their hoorays.

You can travel your whole life through
Or let the whole world come to you.
You will marvel at the faces
Which of their turfs show the traces.

So any given blessed day,
At lunch time, pacing on Broadway,
Side walking downtown N.Y.C.
Catch all the worlds that one can see.

As one moves in this human sea,
This mosaic of ethnicity
Brings out great variety,
A mesh of what the world can be.

For every frown on a forehead,
Every word spoken or just shed,
Every smile a face could provide
Carry a flag planted with pride.

Through these eyes you can see their worlds.
The emblems their accents unfurl
Reveal the greatest mysteries
Of faraway territories…

This world is so full of beauty,
So rich in its diversity
That to see it at any price
Many lifetimes would not suffice.

Life's Recipe

Man Island
Will not stand.
Life's secret
Remains yet
That all men
Stay woven
By sharing
All blessing
And even
Profound pain.
Sorrow shared
Solace paired.
Joy bestowed,
Joy doubled.

Aftermath

Albeit I said to thee I will remain at large,
Deeper within myself I still feel thy presence.
After having endured this crushing experience
My wounded heart offers to thy ghost this adage.

I will, in some corners of my heart, remain thine.
Nothing builds up a man better than his errors.
But it's also grievous to harbor much dolors
Mostly when the latter are dug from just one mine.

Fear not

You hear the great warning
That this world is ending.
You recall John's vision,
Dread the consummation…

There will be after all
Before the great big fall
Whispers meant to inform
You, children, of the storm.

Just like in days of old
His wrath did not unfold
But after His dear ones
Were gathered in at once.

Our loving Father
Forgets us but never.
His way we can't perceive,
His love, cannot conceive.

Therefore in assurance
Celebrate in advance
And we'll see His kingdom,
As He taught us, will come.

He Leadeth me

When in the rising sun I seem to hear His voice
I know that for me He already made a choice
Of the joy that gladdens and sorrow that annoys,
He leadeth me.

Of my weary body that will put up a fight
I feel the lazy screams beneath the morning light
Then I beg on my knees to have some of His might,
He leadeth me.

He leadeth me,
I told my heart to trust in Him facing my sorrow,
He leadeth me,
Then I feel His rain on my meadow

And so I go in the world carrying with me
The love that He bestows, leading me steadily,
I spread it all around despite my misery.

He leadeth me.
When all the doors I knock at are shut in my face,
When all the ones I love seem to shun my embrace
Or with my heavy load I can't keep up the pace,
He leadeth me.

He leadeth me,
Though I don't know whether or not I will see tomorrow,
He leadeth me,
In all my highs and lows this I know.

So as the sun goes down behind the mountain crown
And all the deals I made have only brought me frown,
Peacefully, gracefully, I go lay myself down,
Knowing He leadeth me…

My Beloved Wife

She wakes up in the morning,
Jovial like a bird singing.
It's always a reflection
Of dreams she doesn't mention.

Then shortly she disappears,
Her voice remains in my ears.
So my cloudy mind pictures,
In the bathroom, her gestures.

She emerges from the steam,
Full of vigor as it seems.
The smile brightening her face
Makes me long for her embrace.

Her frail body maneuvers,
Graciously moves and offers
With the light barely dawning
A spectacle worth watching.

She slowly makes arrangements
And revises all garments.
She knows she is monitored,
She performs to be savored.

The few bites of her first meal,
The make-up she applies still,
All carefully enacted,
All lovingly presented.

Then comes the moment sublime.
I close my eyes for my prime.
Tenderly she comes to me,
Her face closing in slowly,

Kisses me repeatedly,
Makes me promise to only
Think of her all through the day.
Then to work she's on her way.

Then I turn over and pray,
Give thanks for days like today
And thinking of tomorrow,
Hope for the same scenario.

A New Dawn

Out of darkest nights, out of darkest fears,
Out of empty lives filled with sorrowful tears,
Out of lonely days with senseless whereabouts,
Out of all the dreams, results of empty shouts,

Out of all failures, all the rights, all the wrongs,
Out of the mistakes designed to make us strong,
Out of all waiting and hoping and searching,
Out of the prayers crowning our despairing,

Out of all kindness, out of all blessings,
Out of the mercies upon us bestowing,
Out of all the Love He shows to His children
Like the sun in the sky dawning from the Eastern.

Nature always tells us to pray for what we need.
Pray the Lord of kindness but don't cradle your greed.
Always when skies are gray and bright smile overdue,
Always, as He promised, appears someone like you.

Out of this large crowd made of friends, made of foes,
Out of memories that in our mind echo,
Just like the dry desert where sprout the fairest lawn
Over our lonely hearts a fair love has just dawned.

Our Song

Ah the little things that life bestows upon us!
The many, merry thrills that in us they create!
Blessed by love given, not searched for, neither bought,
We touched forbidden skies carried upon its wings.

Ah the little things that life bestows upon us!
We both can remain still and let them permeate
The hearts and souls which His divine grace always sought
When we touch hands anew and play angelic strings.

Homeless

Going by aimlessly,
Pushing his carriage-house
He watches dazedly
The good people bustle.
Although many of them
Think of him as a louse,
He has no stratagem
And rather not hustle.

The summer of last year
Was the best of his life.
He had nothing to fear,
Had much more than the means.
In all affairs he dealt
He was sharp as a knife.
He was tall, he was svelte,
Was the king of his queens.

Life decided for him,
So steady and secure,
That in another sphere
He would have to endure.
So the bullet-proof scheme
That he did engineer
Rather than much higher,
Sent him down the ladder.

Even sweet Jessica
For whom he worked so hard,
Forgave not his faux pas.
Though she swore she would stand
Forever by her man,
She left him all haggard.
He could not convince her;
Had no more his treasure,

So down the streets he goes
Looking for a shelter,
Some place that would hinder
The cold piercing his clothes.
Later he'll retire
In the arms of Morpheus.
The cans he'll acquire
Will take him to Bacchus

For only slugs can do,
Alter this suffering,
Drown his brain cells anew,
Take him through this evening.
For watching these people,
Thinking of Jessica
Is dying a little.
Life is not a Soca.

Break up

I could try,

I have tried

To live

My life, your life, their lives

But over and over

Like insidious pain

And nasty April rain

Within me it remain'

That fear,

That chocking sensation

That appears

One clear day

But does not go away.

So I'd sit

And wait, hopeful,

Fearful

But it seems to grow strong.

Before it'd come and go

Now it longs

And little do you know

You're hugging a stranger.
Yes, the eyes,
They just don't recognize
The glow
They did love so.
Love strangers,
Cold, artic cold.
Silence, frigid,
You feel it to the bones.
So you fake,
And she fears
Then she breaks
In her tears.
Misery!
Fissure
Rupture
Departure,
Torture
But the pain
Lingers
And in vain
Others

Offer their place
Their solace
But the traumas reign
And you feign
But it feels so foreign
For you know
Deep inside
That you have to move on
Not prolong
The awkward state of things.
So you let it go
And choose instead to sleep.
Tomorrow,
There is always a tomorrow
Though fearful
You're hopeful
That tomorrow will bring
Solace to everything.

Insecure

And for every heartache,
Every wound, every tear,
With all the love it'll take
I'll chase away your fear.

Never will I forget
That I left you in pain
And I deeply regret
That I tried but in vain

To conceal within me
This surge of doubtfulness
That left you all weary,
In a bedful of stress.

So for every heartache,
Every surge of your fear,
Every day you awake
I'll love you more my dear.

Last Embrace

Of thy sweet room the quiescence
Reveals to me the true essence
Of this deep love I have for thee,
O thou, my beautiful Nancy.

And of thy lips the precious curve
Softly unfolds. What a chef d'oeuvre!
They declare to me loving truths
Anchored so deep within thy youth.

So I delight in your embrace,
Engrave in my mind thy sweet face.
Tomorrow is another day.
Tomorrow, oh please, go away!

"I'm Doing Fine"

If you see on my face
A solitary look
That quickly I displace,
Nosing in an old book,
Don't worry, I'm doing fine.

If in the air I daze
While you're looking so fine,
Utterly unamazed
At the vibes you define,
Don't worry, I'm doing fine.

And if returns the pain,
That born-again sorrow
You feel when I remain
Exchangingly hollow,
Don't worry, I'm doing fine.

See, I didn't lose my grip
And know that I will reap
Just about what I sow
Be it on friend or foe

But if my shortcomings
Cold shoulder my siblings,
In this unfair exchange
Don't think about revenge.

I will eventually,
With your unwavering care,
Unravel finally
The roots of my despair…
Until then, I'm doing fine.

Solitude

At every turn, every corner,
Tomorrow or just whenever,
A silent call to our address
Emerges from our loneliness.

Mysteriously she welcomes us
To encounter the non-obvious
If only we can put aside
The tears of our broken pride.

She comes amid a cluttered room
Filled with the smoke of drunken gloom
To meet the hearts down in the pits
And fondle dejected spirits.

She offers with a placid smile
Promised treasures of a long while
To lovely hearts who have chosen
To give rather than be given.

So she quietly takes her place
And dares not to perturb the race
Of the fragile thoughts entertained
By topsy-turvy minds at hand.

When finally she is noticed
By the victim love has noviced,
Only then she reveals herself
With all the jewels upon her shelf.

But then she rapidly retreats,
Vigilantly takes a back seat
At the least babble that she hears;
Outward sign of deep, teary fears.

She ignores the lack of respect
Displayed by most of her subjects
But still remains the soundless voice
When chance has long run out of choice.

But potentially she remains
The door through all our demands
And works steadily to make real
The many dreams that our hearts, fill.

She brushes aside the first place
Sought by the many of her race.
Rather prefers the reception
Given to her revelations.

Often it is fit to display
Some good, heartfelt graces her way.
After all she only unveils
Of the silence the many tales.

So she edifies all slowly
Whose tears have dried up happily
For only then one encounters
The lasting treasures she offers.

And gradually the big picture,
Beside eyes wide shut, we capture.
And there the smallest of all things
Takes on much wonderful meaning.

For only through our loneliness
And in the realm of quietness
A treasured wisdom is bequeathed
To lonely hearts as blessed gift.

Last Wish

May the hope you invest
Bring you lasting richness
Of health, hope and of wealth,
Well arranged on your shelf.

May the trust you put in
Bring you all blessed things
For to your faith measure
Will be sized your treasure.

May the love that you give
Be the love you receive.
May you give those a chance;
Of life it's the essence.

Your Word

Heaven and Earth will pass; many of us will leave,
But your Word, O my Lord, forever more will live.
It ignites in the hearts of the many chosen,
A fire to entice all the other brethren.

Your unrelenting love never ceases to call.
You've invested too much for Your creatures to fall
For the ever luring gods of their crumbling world
Who astutely offers to them crowns of fake pearls.

You came full of wisdom, of love and forgiveness.
You trod upon this earth, the Father to witness
And every hour spent was to give us Your grace
And every grace received helps us to keep Your trace.

So come divine Master, keep us in Your embrace.
Help us, loving Savior, help us to keep Your pace
For heaven, earth will pass, many of us will leave
Unless Your strong Spirit helps us Your word retrieve.

A Part of God, a Part of Me

And after all the lights are dimmed
I retire from this long day.
Since tomorrow plans are all trimmed
My mind freely just strolls away.
Thirty days since I heard the news
That ever since made me happy.
It comes each morning with its cues;
A part of God's growing in me.

I know I felt this once before
It seems almost ten years ago.
It marvels me as an encore
Though now he's almost a macho.
Now peacefully I feel within
This feeling of perfect accord
Brought to me by this life growing
As part of me and part of God.

Over the years he grew handsome
Though to me he's still my baby.
I pray that he's given wisdom
So in this life he'll be happy.
I still feel the beats of my heart
When I hear, "I love you Mommy".
He has been from the very start
A part of God, a part of me.

So to my tiny vital spark
That I treasure oh so dearly
I hold these queries in the dark
Revealing how much I worry.
What will be of your tomorrow?
Will you be handsome or pretty?
Will you know joy or know sorrow,
Be more part of God than of me?

There will be time for you to grow,
Time of game and time of nipple,
Time that will fly like an arrow
Causing your young years to triple.
But deep in the warmth of my nest,
This safe, loving, maternal pod,
I promise to give you my best,
You, part of me and part of God.

In small bundle we receive love
That rearranges all our deals.
It's a blessing sent from above
Whose mystery our souls, chills.
But for tonight as I linger
With my eyes foggy and dreamy,
To hold in my arms I hunger,
This part of God, this part of me.

Who Loves You?

One enchanted evening he saw your lovely face
And ever since he walks steadily in your trace.
He always longs to hear
Your laughter and your fears
To set as an echo
Of his heart the tempo…
The one whose world crumbles again
When from him your hand you regain,
Who counts the minutes when you're gone,
Stifling, cause you left him alone
Whose time flies when his hand you hold,
Laughs at your jokes mimicked or told,
Who marvels at your sparkling eyes
For in them his sun dares to rise,
Who longs for your tender embrace,
Yet strong all his fears to erase.
The one who each and every morn
Wakes up gladly just to adorn
A smile for the world to reveal
That of his world you're the queen still.

Central Park Scene

Two people sitting on a bench,
Two faces that the teardrops drench,
One nodding occasionally,
One speaking too vehemently.

The orange ball piercing the trees
Transforms the ground in foreign seas.
It did its chores again today,
Gave lots of warmth for birds to play.

Vaguely you hear the City's voice
Brought by the wind given the choice
To bounce against the tall windows
Or rockabye baby swallows…

Two people sitting on a bench
With faces that still teardrops drench,
Now kissing emotionally,
Speaking much less vehemently.

Daydream

I dream of a country
With sun of golden rays
Where the birds on the trees
Would sing their jolly praise.
I'd take you by the hand on a roadless meadow,
We'd circle aimlessly, never feeling the glow
Of the beams of sunlight,
With silky impression,
That though sunny and bright
Would instill us passion.

I dream of a country
Immense and measureless,
'T plays the "Great" symphony
When the wind comes impress
On every living soul the blessed warmth of day
And offers jolly rides over mounts, over bay.
And the sea and the skies
With matching tint of blue
Would reveal to your eyes
The love I have for you…

Then deep within my mind
I kiss your lovely face.
Leaving my world behind
I reach this lovely place
Where the look in your eyes, the sweetness of your voice,
Your jolly gentleness telling me to rejoice,
Remind my festive heart
Of this country for two,
This heaven set apart,
This wonder world of you.

The Garden of my Soul

The garden of my soul is a lonely meadow
Where spring up many buds made of joy and sorrow.
Flowers of many kinds adorn its peaceful maze
Though much of weeds and thorns so disrupt their arrays.
Birds of different attire sing tunes of jolly air
But crows of somber coats startle you here and there.
The days can be sunny, foggy, rainy or cold
But the nights, though pleasant, keep their stories untold.
The winds, they come and go but never reveal twice
The same lessons to learn, the same heartfelt advice.

The trees they planted there have deep-rooted the soil.
They can sustain the worst of a lifetime turmoil.
They grew with poverty but with sheer tenderness,
They grew with faith and love so to the world confess
The helpers' skillful works, the Gardener's taste of choice,
All faithful listeners of the Landowner's voice.

Many people trespassed, many strangers wandered.
Still many came with plans, their own seeds they offered
But the winds of springtime had them scattered away
Into other meadows where they grew come what may.
But some have left their trace of lovely trees with shades
And over and over, all through my life's decades,
I miss their aromas, their essence of flowers,

The breeze they stopped blowing on my warmest hour.
The garden of my soul is still open today,
Greeting passing strangers, pleading with them to stay.
But deep within its soil it harbors the secret
That of its span of years the best is to come yet.
So to the birds and crows, the flowers and the thorns,
The sunny days of spring or the cold winter morns,
To the lovely stranger come to settle a score,
To the one who returns like a blessed encore,
To the workers who shed selflessly sweat and tears
And the loving Gardner following what He hears
I say thanks from my heart to have made as a whole,
With inputs of all kinds, the garden of my soul.

My Early Friends

I wander whatever happened to your faces,
If time with its brushes, painter for all races,
Put lines on your profiles, of wisdom or of rage?
Are you rich and famous, alive or held hostage
By those younger year hooks of trip to the ether
Caused by the volatile or some foreign liquor.

Are you still in a maze wondering if should you try
Not to live nonchalant, watching time pas you by,
Raising a family, caring for your elders
Or wishing they would die and leave you some treasures?
Are you in some country with sun, snow or unrest,
Are you just lying there with the soil on your chest?

Forgive the crude nature, the array of choices
Of questions I debate recalling your voices.
Though God alone decides where we spring, grow and die,
I often wish once more we'd eat from the same pie.
Wherever you may be, I hope you're in God's hands
For time and time again I miss my early friends.

Lord Jesus

For having loved us before Your time
Lord Jesus, we love You.
For having said yes to the Father,
Lord Jesus, we worship You.
For Your birth on that cold night,
Lord Jesus, we adore You.
For serving us in Your younger years,
Lord Jesus, we thank You.
For the teachings You give us,
Lord Jesus, we uphold You,
For Your tiring walks on this Earth,
Lord Jesus we bless You.
For bearing our hearts of stone,
Lord Jesus we glorify You,
For Your agony in Gethsemane
Lord, please, can we watch with You?
For knowing in advance the nature of your sufferings,
Lord Jesus, we praise you.
For yet handing Yourself over,
Lord we offer ourselves to You.
For carrying Your cross to Your death,
Lord, thanks for showing us the way.
For Your rising and Your ascension,
Lord Jesus, open us the gate.
For the Spirit You send us,
Master, please, remain with us always.
Remember, Remember

Remember, my jolie,

Remember endlessly,
Remember how swiftly
Love came crashing in us.
How the Lord I adore,
Unlike ever before,
Sent it down to the shore
Of hearts He made pious.

We were poor and lonely,
Lacking of this jolly
Blessing He usually
Bestows upon the Earth.
And we wore as a crown,
Of the burden the frown
And at times we felt down,
Deprived of divine mirth.

Remember how lightly
We became suddenly,
Ridded of misery.
We became radiant
And were as they define,
Strolling upon cloud nine
That moment the Divine
Made us norm-defiant.

Remember, remember,
I told you thereafter
That they will not linger,
Trying to spoil our bliss.
Remember, remember
That over and over
They will come and offer
Fake pearls so to dismiss

This treasure that we found,
Relentlessly will pound
At what Heaven has bound
Until it's no longer.
Remember I told you
What we will have to do
To keep this love brand new
And remind each other

How love can be fragile
And easily defiled
Unless we both defile
In the tracks of our Lord.
For unless we abide,
Under His wings go hide,
Despising human pride,
He'll shun our accord.

Remember, remember,
I love you forever,
Remember don't waver,
My godsent, my soul mate.

...And I Love You Too

There will forever be upon this rolling world,
From all the hearts pounding for all these lovely pearls,
There will be rolling down, from pens of every tongue,
Loving words to express feelings that come along.

Some of them will reveal very bestial aspects,
They will be degrading, bluntly lacking respect.
Other will come to you favoring angel rhyme,
Moving deep within you the spirit anytime.

There is always a poem, an arrangement of words
That brings to your palate feelings so far unheard.
You ponder their sources, dream their inspiration,
But they remain unique, clenching their distinction.

The love you can afford is the one you dream of.
The love you dream about comes to you from above.
For if you dream of it, you also hope for it,
Since hoping is praying, you wait for the spirit.

For only from above will come the blessed love.
The one's that here to stay, that remains unheard of.
It comes to you swiftly, as does the breath of life,
Steps right into your world, settles your inner strife.

And like the lucky ones, you're caught in the whirlwind,
This mother tornado sweeps you up for a spin.
Carried upon her wings and thrilled by her joy rides,
You become addicted, refuse to leave her sides.

So again and again lovely ballads you'll hear
Singing of the strong love also the inner fears
That follow when the heart, unsteady in its core,
Regains the blissful grace it enjoyed once before.

For loving to the heart is water to the fish,
Like prayer to the soul, it can never finish.
There will forever be since my dream has come true,
Loving words to express the love I have for you.

The Love we Share

The love we share was born one day,
Resulting of the painful ways,
The sun, with its relentless rays,
Tries to the moon its love, convey.

Daily from the east to the west,
Radiating its heat at its best,
It lengthens its path in protest
Of her perpetual lack of zest.

And so the stars in unison
Came to this blessed decision
To send the bliss of this union
To some earthly destination.

It sneaked upon us one sweet eve
And hid itself, master of thieves,
Among the bang so exclusive
Of magic July forth festive.

So there we stood in steady awe,
Stricken down by this blessed draw
And in each other's eyes we saw
This cosmic bliss fallen and raw.

So call it serendipitous,
A magic tale, lame ludicrous,
The love that we share among us
Will strike the world as fictitious.

But as long as the sun will shine
And bathe the world with golden lines
Under the watch of love divine
We will remain, your hand in mine.

My Maiden

I love a beautiful maiden.
With her love she can ease my pain.
I love a beautiful maiden
With love steady as a refrain.

With her smile of heavenly pearl
She can settle the fiercest score.
See how her lovely arms unfurl
To give hugs and kisses galore.

Take away the air that I breathe
Along with the warmth of sunrays,
My choice your palate may deceive
But don't take my maiden away.

The Love I Have for You

The love I have for you
Remains a mystery.
It's nothing déjà vu.
It's soul refinery.

I feel it intensely
When you're at my side.
It chokes me dreadfully
When from my eyes you hide.

It has total power
Over my poor being,
Chooses to devour
Of my heart every string.

It leaves me no recess,
No rest when I'm weary.
It demands nothing less
Than my soul to flurry.

For my nights have no dream
That doesn't start with you
And my days they all seem
A fairy tale come true.

You are my light of days,
The stillness of my nights.
You, with your lovely rays,
Secure my spirit's flights.

The love I have for you
Forever I'll cherish
For where there's life, there's you,
Without you I'll perish.

My Beloved Mother

Just before He renders
His Soul to expire,
He turned to His brothers,
Set His Heart on fire.

Despite His sufferings
And the world's unbelief,
He made this offering
To the ones left in grief.

"John, this is your Mother",
He said to him, in pain.
Oh what a sweet treasure!
Kinship we then obtained.

"Woman, behold your son"
He said to her after.
Ever since she took on
The task of our Mother.

For a Mother she is,
Pointing always the way
To her Son's love and His
Laws for us to obey.

Sweet Mother, we love you,
Pure virgin, pray for us
That in this world snafu
We remain right and just.

Show unto us, we pray,
Your sweet and humble way
So that we may someday
See God's face in display.

Daughter of the Father,
Spouse of God, the Spirit,
Mother of the Savior,
God's handmaid tripartite.

Without You

From the depths of my lonely soul
I long for you to make me whole.
The thoughts of you that linger on
Give me rainbows to glide upon.
I dip my mind ov' and over
In the souvenirs you offer.

But all the while my empty stare
Docks the shore of an isle so fair;
Your lovely face, which tries to hide,
With a smile where my fate abides,
The promise of a me-and-you,
The certainty of love brand new.

Unceasingly your realm of love
Draws in my soul so deprived of
Its mere essence of survival.
There, longing for your arrival
I dream of golden tomorrows
That'd make amend for my sorrow.

Through mountains high and valleys low
I will seek you my sweet sparrow.
We will rekindle the blessing
That by your absence is stifling,
Making my dreams of future bliss
A happy scene hard to dismiss.

From the depths of my weary soul
I beg of you, come take control
Of this ship drifting aimlessly,
Of this heart racing painfully.
For in this dark and icy land
I yearn for the warmth of your hand.

Lost Soul

In the dark alleys of my night
I call your name with voice of fright.
As though to save my frantic soul
I search and search for you to hold.

The dreadful feeling nursing me
Reaps from my soul pure misery.
It pronounces the verdict cold
That right before my eyes unfolds;

The days to come will bring to me
Painful burden of infamy
But in the depth of my cold night
I miss the warm glow of your sight.

Painfully it dawns in my mind
That you willfully left behind
This vengeful curse to abrade me,
Me and my loathed polygamy.

For when you came in to my life
You chased away my inner strife,
Brought me your smile, brought me your love
And the blue sky from God above.

So I relentlessly pursue
This trail of love, this shade of blue
But mercilessly I come back
Time and again on my first track.

There, in this terrifying maze,
Deprived of the least of sunrays,
The stampede felt within my chest
Favors a derby at its best.

So many times your sunlight rose
Upon my mind which long time froze,
Your lovely bouquet, which lingers
To underline all my errors.

And the free fall that never ends
While I desperately seek your hands,
Proclaims aloud from land to sea
That your brown eyes I'll never see.

And suddenly I come to grip
That what I sow is what I reap
And though for you I now hunger
I'll enjoy your sweet smile never.

Oh I lost your silky shadow
In this maze of columns and rows,
I lost my heart that followed you,
"See", you would say, " Didn't I tell you?"

But I cling to my emptiness
Of love, blue sky and your caress
For this whole world of nothingness
For ever seals my cursedness…

So if you see through your window
A lonely wandering shadow
That seems not to know where to go
Don't you go laugh at its sorrow.

For the dark alleys of my night,
Where I holler with voice of fright
Portray my soul resting in shroud
While still calling your name out loud.

Nightfall

Steadily and serene over Mother Nature
The shadows of the day transform the vale feature.
Like a deer to water, the mighty king of noon
Bows down to his loved one, retires much too soon.

From grateful nightingales you hear evening prayers,
Of heavens' canopy light up many glitters.
And of the old church bells, the chime almost joyous
Sounds all over the land the blessed Angelus.

Serene and steadily, with a smile on his face,
The prince of shining stars lovingly comes embrace
His bride already robed in somber lingerie;
Happy to have one night again with his chérie.

The melodious stream meeting its destiny,
In the dark waves of sea expires hopelessly.
Its sorrowful good byes, like a repeated call,
Account for the mournful echo of the nightfall.

Rain

I love the drifting rain
On window pane
Tapping down the sorrow
On us below,
Dripping lonely teardrops
On yellow hops.

I love the thunderous rain,
Roaring in vain
With crackling of lightning
To us showing
The vengeance of the clouds,
Spreading shrouds.

I love the misty rain
Like children,
At sweet voice of mother
They gesture.
It dries at the first gleam
Of sunbeam.

October rain, slowly falling,
Annoying,
Spreading dullness and gloom
Like a tomb
Over the soul's hopeless
Joyfulness.

The Master's Embrace

Like the sunlight dawning over the dark blue sea,
Like the flower budding from a green slender stalk,
Like a geyser springing for stunning eyes to see,
Like the long expected of your baby's first talk,
Subtle and astounding is the Master's embrace.

Like the knock of a friend when you're so down and out,
Like a free, friendly ride when you miss the last bus,
Like a sweet mother's smile to a rude toddler's pout,
A favorable verdict that took months to discuss,
Swift and reconstructing is the Master's embrace.

Like the loveliest meal after a rigid lent,
A darling baby girl after a long labor,
A remorseful sinner given chance to repent,
The latest bestseller of your favorite author,
Gentle and fulfilling is the Master's embrace.

With no kind of warning it reaches to your shore.
It permeates your soul down to its smallest pore,
Enthralls your meek spirit into a blissful whirl,
Leaving you strong and weak with your heart in a swirl.

Like a sudden pardon obtained on death-row eve,
When at last she shows up while you thought she would not,
Like your first taste for life when for so long you grieved,
Like meeting a loved one who lingered in your thoughts,
Always with no warning is the Master's embrace.

Our Seasons

Just like the spring
My love spreads wings
Over the nature of your heart.
Just like the spring,
Precious feelings
Set us both for a brand new start.

Just like summer
My soul hovers,
Melting in the heat of your love.
Just like summer
My heart lingers
Like the haze from the sky above.

Just like the fall
At your mere call
I'd shed my covers just for you.
Just like the fall
And through it all
The colors of our love are true.

Just like winter
I will offer
The purest sound my heart can sing
For in winter
Or whenever
Your love brings me the warmth of spring.

My Secret

I'm gonna tell you a secret,
A secret kept deep within me.
I'm gonna tell you a secret
That in my eyes you may not see.

I'm gonna share you my secret,
My heart wrenching of confession.
I'm gonna share you my secret
And trust in your good intention.

But let me sit and hold your hand
For my heart often skips a beat.
When around you it can't pretend
To behave every time we meet.

I'm gonna tell you a secret,
A secret I hope you don't share.
I'm gonna tell you my secret
If one day I finally dare.

To Pray, To Love

I always wonder
Every time I pray,
Why my heart jitters,
Drifting down your way.

Every time I yearn
For my dear Savior,
Slowly I discern
You in my mirror.

As He once taught me
If I come to Him
I would learn slowly
To love without scheme.

My poor heart He trains
To vibrate like His,
Gently He sustains
My bundle of His.

So if when I pray
My heart bleeds for you
Gratefully I say
Jesus, I love you.

P.S. The heart is like a wild beast;
When finally it finds its prey,
It loves it until death.

If Tomorrow

For a long time I will carry
The scar of this damn misery
Crushing my soul, body and mind
With no solace of any kind.

I gave you all I had inside
Knowing that soon you'd be my bride
But your plans did not include me,
You walked away with no mercy.

You had to show your entourage
That you could fulfill your presage;
Since you had my heart as a whole,
You took my mind, body and soul.

Like a beast out of her dive
You had to feed your inner drive.
But I will go my lonely way
Trying to conceal my dismay.

You'll go bragging to every friend
How you and I came to an end.
And in no time you will promote
Another victim to denote.

He will wear his heart on his sleeve
To offer you, daughter of Eve.
But deep inside, I am the same,
The fires of anger I tamed.

If you decide, you never know
To return to me tomorrow,
I'll surely fall in your embrace,
Too happy to find my solace
And tenderly I'll make query
About my mind, soul and body.

Love

I'm no expert on the matter
But even so I will utter
This thought of wisdom;
One is never empty handed
When in cradle love was planted
Right in his bosom.

Love remains the utmost feeling,
Joy and suffering I can bring
To every creature.
Love is always self-offering,
In so doing joy-receiving;
Its only pleasure.

Love is the foundation of peace,
The one who does not love will miss
His serenity.
You see them pacing down the streets,
Treating everybody they meet
With hostility.

For without love the heart suffers,
Loses its inner drive, withers;
Lacking its essence.
It does not receive the blessing
Of Heaven that should be causing
Its effervescence.

So naturally one wonders;
All these suicides and murders
Will they end one day?
Love is the only solution,
Love can bring the world's salvation,
Chasing fears away.

Love is the miracle of all,
Making us answer to the calls
Of the ones in need.
Love is the greatest of healers,
The quintessence of elixirs;
Our souls it feeds.

So let us turn to our Father,
Begging Him over and over
That He enriches
Us creatures made at His image
But who remain bound as hostage
Of this world riches.

Love one another steadily,
Love one another faithfully
As He still loves us.
They will recognize at this sign
That we had left the world behind
To follow Jesus.

He is the way, the truth, the life,
Who puts an end to the big strife
Between love and hate
And if we follow what He says
We'll find ourselves one of these days
Within the Heavens' pearly gate.

The Secret

The grievance we hold on to
In our bosom
Shuts the door at the Lord who
Works for His kingdom.

Cast away the trespasses
Done by your brethren,
The Lord will bestow graces
Unto you. Amen!

Preamble

There they stood exchanging
Highlights of life stories.
One talking, one weighing
Downfalls against follies…

"From all the empty days,
The painful sacrifice,
Is it cautious to say
Go ahead, don't think twice?

"Dreaming of so much more,
Meeting the criteria,
Or just a plain encore
Of empty euphoria…

"In this stable pattern
Of failing the basics,
Is it wise to discern
The traits of lunatics?"

So they walked exchanging
But failed to understand
That in higher dealings
Their souls walk hand in hand.

Quite Suddenly

In all of a sudden
On that September morn,
That ton of a burden
Deep in our hearts was born.

The sun was there, shining
On that promising day
And on all living things
The blessings of its rays.

The traffic in a rush
As it does so often
Never pictured that such
Would be their realm of pain.

And all of a sudden
The world came tumbling down.
I'll tell you my dear friend,
It was all dusty brown.

You can spend a lifetime
Chewing upon this day
You will not have a dime
Of sense coming your way…

They must have thought it well;
It was so organized.
The devil failed to tell
Them that they'd be chastised.

For sure within their minds
They thought of reprisal,
A measure that would find
Match for this upheaval.

Call them senseless or fools,
Fanatics, extremists,
To me they were just tools
Of that big con artist.

And so our rolling world
Will again have to face
A mind twisted and twirled
That it'll have to efface.

But since there is always
From the worst happenings
A strong message that says
To us much vital things,

Let us reconsider
Upon this God's green Earth
How we can make better
The plight of foreign turf…

Often when neglected
A child deprived of love,
Despite what's expected,
His older brother, shoves.

My Daughter

From the glass wall I contemplate
The meek angel sent not too late.
Her frail body shivers, weakened,
Shakes repeatedly from the pain
She endured coming down to us
From that divine land of Jesus.

Selfishly I want her to stay
Though in her cries I hear her say,
"What have I done, what got in' me,
Why return to this misery?"
-"My dear treasure, it was your choice
To come once more with us rejoice
In God's greatness of creations
And proclaim His love to nations."

P.S.

Life remains after all a gift from God above,
The way we live this life, in return, shows our love.

Remain Still

So I remain still,
Master, not knowing what to ask.
But I sit at your feet and fast…
An awesome feeling transforms me
For my soul bathes in Your mercy.
Its dim and trembling flame once more today regained,
Brightened by You, the crave to love You Lord again.
There I remain still…
So the sublime pleasure
Of Your presence in me
Reveals the true nature
Of You I cannot see.
My poor self glorifies Your Name,
The might of Your hand I acclaim
And contemplate the world with eyes rendered brand new.
Around me I see signs of the wonder of You.
Remain in me, my Lord; never of me let go,
Show me Your tenderness so I can be also
Reflection of the One, who rekindles my soul,
Dwells within me always, fills me and makes me whole.
And I'll remain still…

Three Little Flowers

When I was six years old, one day I fell in awe
Before the loveliness of a few white flowers.
They had lately budded. They were fresh, moist and raw,
Had just sprung to the light, free of sunlight showers.

I stood admiring their petal purity
Unable to pinpoint to what likening them.
To the simplest of hearts, the soul's virginity,
Angelic hymn of praise, the purest diadem.

Hurriedly I took them to the presbytery
With intent to present as a meek offering,
Simply as reverence to my Mother Mary;
It was the month of May, so dear to her offspring.

So I went to the priest, the flowers to entrust.
He took them smilingly with no hesitation
Then told me, "My dear child", after counting them first,
"One precious is missing from this veneration."

I remained all puzzled thinking where did the priest
Could have possibly seen the buds of my garden…
So in reply I said: "Father, if you insist
Tomorrow, when it sprouts, I'll bring the other then."

Early the next morning for church I did depart
To bring the last flower of my little garden.
But the priest looked at me: "My child, without your heart
Your oblation remains lovely but yet barren.

"These gorgeous petals will soon fade and then wither.
Only one will always safeguard its purity.
Bring before the altar of your loving Mother
Your heart, my loving child, in all of its beauty."

All my life you were my model
O chaste Mother of my Savior.
If ever I've lost my gospel,
Please, pray my Lord in my favor.

To this day even more
I offer my meek heart
To the Lord I adore
Who made me from the start.

Lovely flowers only
His altar can garnish
Souls of great purity
His Heaven embellish.

A Man

A man
Once had a dove
Just plain
But full of love.
He thought
In righteousness
Let's not
Live in a mess.
So he
Opened the door.
Slowly
What he lived for
Freely
Took her first flight
Sadly
Left him in plight.

Took time
For him to assess;
His prime
Was queen of his chess.
Alone
With his emptiness
In prone
His face in distress
He prayed

For the Lord's goodness.
He lay
Waiting to be bless'.
Maybe
He thought to himself
Will she
My sweet little elf
Return
To her lovely nest
Not spurn
But revive my zest.

Junie,
O my sweet queen of heart,
Chérie,
You have torn it apart,
Truly
The day you did depart.
You are
The sole cause of my joy,
You are
The grace He once deploy',
You are
My true essence of life,
By far
My other, better half.

The Blackstone's

There goes H.M. Blackstone,
Strolling through Yellowstone,
Admire her strong prance,
Her stride, what an offence!

Now here J.C. Blackstone,
Talking on his cellphone,
Full of his quantity,
Emphatic quality.

He shouts to her and said,
"I am a man, obey!
Created I was first,
Due to respect and trust."

-"But no my dear J.C.,
Be honest and you'll see,
I am a man at best,
This, my kids manifest.

"See you're only a man
But I am a wo-man
With a womb I was set
Your failings to offset."

And opinions were sown,
Words by words overthrown,
Mostly by anger fed,
Retaliated with stead.

The punches kept coming
But they saw not the scene;
Their jaguar by some teen
Was being stolen clean.

They ran and screamed out loud,
Classy style put in shroud,
Desperately attempting
To get their belonging.

Exhausted, worn out,
This sudden workout
Brought back to this couple
Forgotten health trouble.

H. M., her torn ankle
That got her disable
Some long, long time ago,
Working in her stable

J. C., his lungs weakened
By some fine cigar brand.
So she went on hoping
And he, loudly wheezing.

Helping one another
They went on thereafter
Seeing that together
They were much less weaker.

Funny how misery
Experienced suddenly
Brings about unity
And blessed harmony.

Storm

One of those summer nights of sky hostility,
When thunder, clouds, lightning and all of the above
Seem to fight to conquer some celestial trophy
And make tremble of fright every body they shove.

One of those summer nights when the sky is in rage
And of the storm you feel the wind and its toughness.
They blow mercilessly, making sudden wreckage,
Even the frightened sky wears a veil of darkness,

You can see in the air, flying from all over,
Numerous pairs of wings rushing to take cover.
Of an early mourning heaven become bearer
And this sudden dusk makes Mother Nature somber.

The shadows penetrate every place but my heart.
It remains strong facing this cataclysmic gloom
Coming from who knows where, spreading in every part
Boredom, increasing fright, just like a day of doom.

Within my heart, my Lord, You remain ever strong.
Gaiety and gentleness, hope and tranquility
You bring to Your servant. So whenever among
Tribulations he bides under Your care only.

And the storm went raging…Peace remained within me.
Alone in my room I direct to You Father,
My soul, my self, my thoughts and just as suddenly
I feel deep within me the warmth of Your Power.

When it's all Over

Say, how can I go on? Please, tell me what to do.
How can I go unwrap my heart from around you?
The mere thought of a night spent ahead without you
Has a bitter taste of judgment-day rendez-vous.
It brings a sense of doom, of unending nightmare,
Of toddler who lost mom in a crowd of big fair…
And I will miss your smile…
Oh say you'll stay a while.

I know he waits for you; I know you just can't wait
But in your escapade you used my heart as bait.
I just can't realize how selfish you became.
My worming leaves you cold, and you eyes are the same.
You want to be my friend; we can have lunch sometimes,
You will call me, you said. Oh don't you waste your dime.
Nothing can ease your wile
When your trunk's in the aisle.

But now I remember, it hits me suddenly
Those times when you would sit for hours silently.
I could not get a word from your too anxious face
While from my quarantine I longed for your embrace
But if you keep saying that it is all over
And feel that we cannot be an item ever
Although I love you more than any words can say,
I will, if you insist, never stand in your way.

You came into my life and taught me how to live.
You saved me from my cell; my loneliness took leave.
You kissed my fears away and I saw my sunrise
Each time, on my poor self, you set your lovely eyes.
But you say that heartbreak never killed anyone
And that I should be strong and date other someone,
That there've been many miles
Between us for a while.

You should just leave instead, don't look for alibi.
Don't go show sympathy because you see me cry.
I'll pick up the pieces you shattered all over,
I 'll write you love verses with more soul, more fever,
Treating of a new world made just for me and you
Where nothing comes to life unless you want it to
And where you would just smile
For more than just a while.

To my Lord Jesus

All my life, my dear Lord,
I've loved you immensely
And tried to come aboard
Your big arch of mercy.

Just like at Your command
Noah took them by pairs,
You led them by the hands,
Dealt Your Father's affairs.

You showed them peacefully
The Source of their beings,
Taught them relentlessly
To bear their sufferings.

I thank You Lord Jesus,
Out of that big sea,
Though so many of us
That You have chosen me.

All my life, my dear Lord,
I've loved You immensely,
All my days left on board
I'll serve You faithfully.

"Dark September Day"

In this world of ours, always at a great price,
Expressions of strong love come from big sacrifice.
It seems to always say to the wondering mind
That only through painful efforts solace we find.
See the love of mothers after children are born;
You'd never guess they just had their viscera torn.
Their serene, peaceful look of accomplished labor
Reflects the inner sense of love that they savor.
It seems that to obtain the goals for which we yearn
A painful price we'll pay with lessons to be learn'.

In this world of ours, like kids we never learn.
God as a good Father, though merciful, is stern.
Since from the day of old He preached of His Kingdom,
By necessary means He'll work for it to come…
Never in history has it ever occurred,
In this world, so much love, from so many hearts spurred.
As if it were all stored in those two tall buildings
Of the richest City, all freed on that morning.
And the so many souls released by these fires
Will be in history called modern day martyrs.

In this world of ours, after much painful mourn,
Maybe we'll capture groups of the ones to be scorned.
But we should never go insensitive and cold
Lest our dear beloved ones, our martyrs miss their goal.
Oh they show us the way: for fellow human beings
And for a better world, they forsook everything.
So love one another: it's still the same lesson
Challenging us from then till 2021.
In this world of ours, world of precious freedom,
Let us within our hearts freely choose His Kingdom.

For in that world of His, so just in everything,
They will have no more qualms and no more suffering.
Though to our standard they might have been short-changed,
They'll give them lovingly golden crowns in exchange.
They'll look down upon us, mourn our unbelief
That their big sacrifice would have failed to relieve.
And this Earth of ours, like a big rolling ball,
Will go crushing martyrs who in her bosom fall…
Will we ever fathom, without Heaven's advice
Why every ounce of love's woven to sacrifice?

What a Feeling!

Who would have thought in my lifetime
That it would come slowly to this,
This ever living love of rhyme
That feels my heart with treasured peace?

In the stillness of my quarters,
Apart from the cries of the town,
I can ponder on all matters
That I carry under my crown.

Only the ticking of a clock
Gives to my thinking a measure,
A measure steady as a rock,
A metronome for my leisure.

There I would go on for hours
And sturdily between the lines,
My pen the paper, devours
To reveal thoughts that are not mine.

Nevertheless it's exciting
To write down what's given to you.
It unveils, among other things,
Of your muse the character too.

So I'd write miles and miles of thoughts
To make a point, describe a site
But my mind only remains caught
In the choice of words that I cite.

I forewarn, admonish, counsel,
Keeping eyes on my metering
And I strip my heart a little,
Striving to be disconcerting.

Even in my early slumber
When Morpheus opens fiestas
I fight to keep myself sober
To write one or two more stanzas.

The part that the most entertains,
That I somewhat anticipate,
Is to read the goal I obtained,
See if it pleases my palate.

But if it did, right then I reap
The joy to have brought to their end,
'Gainst Morpheus mythical leap,
The strophes, which my wake, sustained.

To fill my heart with treasured peace,
Who would have thought in my lifetime
That to get a feeling like this
I'd have recourse to verse and rhyme?

33RD Avenue

The rusty glare of evening sun
Reflects the mood of this here crowd;
The people walk, the traffic runs,
All trapped in this thick, dusty cloud.

Alone, counting her every step,
A young girl walks, sad and haggard.
The clothes she wears long lost their pep
But this detail she disregard.

And this old man handles his pan
To prospected donors chosen
But too swiftly they all pretend
To look away much too often.

The warmer air blowing inland
Tickles your nose with camellia.
At times your senses they offend,
At times it's snuffed anesthesia.

And silently the glare gets dimmed
Then turns into a shade of brown.
The blinding sphere that it once seemed
For today will cause no more frown.

And so the day closes curtains,
The sun to its room retires.
The neon lights now entertain
The many ones boredom tires.

So night sets in with its own tricks
And life takes a brand new meaning
Where walking cool and talking slick
Is more useful than demeaning.

On and off comes the gentle breeze
Bringing up the beat of the town
And the camellia scented tease
In fair exchange is carried down.

The traffic fires seem to compete
With the cadence of Christmas lights;
To every flow of the side streets
The red avenue shows its might.

And here and there a few shoppers
Tread in and out of fancy stores.
They run cross against the bumpers
From fear of missing a décor.

But suddenly you hear the sound
Of a red hook and ladder truck
Emerging and quickly south bound
To some gathering out of luck.

Added to this noise pollution

Surges a screeching sound of tires.
Arms fly in gesticulation,
Expressing silent words of fire.

And so it goes, and it echoes,
The dying beat of the City,
Cascading to a steady close,
Slowly taming its night fury.

You can just sit if you so please
And passively enjoy the scene
Or if it makes you more at ease
You can come and just mingle in.

But either way the avenue
To the true free spirit in town
Will offer more than just a hue
But also scents and surround sound.

So if ever you're feeling blue,
Lacking of zest, empty or sad,
Come enjoy, experience anew
The latest style, the recent fad.

For on 33rd Avenue
Where traffic runs and people walk,
There'll be a theme for someone who
Despite any gloom can crowd stalk.

Advent

And gradually the sun has become much tender
And the tree losing leaves ask in sheer decency,
"Why this change in weather, is it fall already,
Is it the season when hearts to love surrender?"

So nature put at ease, shouts like a messenger,
And heralds the love theme sung by angels only.
The soul perceives the chime and retells the story
Of that winter night of the birth in a manger.

Do you know why the rays of the sun have golden,
Why this loving feeling in the hearts of all men?
It's because Heaven's Host of a stable made choice.

Therefore heaven and earth expectantly rejoice.
Echoing the message, the moon and stars glimmer,
The world upon its knees awaits the Redeemer.

To my Babyliscious Ant

If one day we drift apart,
I can honestly say I will cease to exist.
If one day we drift apart
I will lose of this life even the will to live.

From the earliest days that we came to be one
You've always touched my soul in a very strange way.
Yes I say you're different, unique, so uncommon
That with you I became what I could never be.

It's always the result of a long awaiting
Filled with patience, dark days and gloomy solitude,
It's always, as I said, after the darkest nights
That comes shiny and new
Somebody just like you.

Have I ever told you how truly blest I feel
When I look in your eyes just before you kiss me?
Have I ever told you how contented and still
I become when your lips on my face take a stroll?

I could die, I could die. Nothing could ever spoil
The bliss that fills me in when caught within your arms.
But you mentioned soul mate. Do you really mean it?
Are you just using words ignoring their meanings,

Or do you just like me internalize the thrill
That one I experience at each and every time
Your voice, the words you say, your face, your lovely eyes,
Your hands, your tender lips, your feet, my favorite prize,
Anything that's from you come to caress my soul?

I will never find words to explain to this world
The feel I hold within caused by you in my world.
I am made so brand new,
I have reached other skies.
No wonder without you
Why I feel so chastised.

You always stroke in me chords I thought didn't exist
And seem to know too clearly the things to say that'd
Make me all warm inside.

Yes, I love you baby, if that can encompass
This divine excitement surging deep within me
When with your own sweet ways you come and set your eyes
Upon my poor being. For then I realize
That yes, as you mentioned, from the get go,
The first, the early days,
Looking into your eyes I had found my soulmate,
My other half.

To a Lovely Stranger

(In an empty airport hall)

If I see you lovely
But remain steadily
Hushed up
Maybe you'll understand
Not think that he's just plain
Stuck up.
What I wish I could say
Remains along the way
Choked up
But I want you to know
You're the star of my show;
Wise up.

You and I

I will sing, I will sing of the love you bring me
For you will always stroke the cords of my guitar.
The guitar of my heart, ignored by so many,
Whose strings of secret love remained untouched so far.

Remain the sole player who skillfully transmits
The jolly airs bringing cheerful glow to my face.
Together you and I, minds, bodies and spirits,
We will remain secured in this divine embrace.

Birthday Wishes

So now today is your birthday!
One step closer to old and gray,
Or so you think, come on, admit,
You'll soon trade your steak for some grits…
But all the while
With a bright smile
You go around spreading your joy,
Kindness and love always deploy
To every one crossing your path.
When times are rough, you make them laugh…
Well, in return
Just cause you learned
Of this life the true meaning,
I will grant you the following:
Long life with true friends all around,
Good health with feet strong on the ground.
Even if health from you depart,
I'll grant you love to warm your heart.

Cheer up

I can attempt to make you see
The light behind your misery.
I can offer words to lessen
The blue feeling caused by your pain.
But nothing will fill the vacuum
Left in our hearts by a fewsome.

See, hearts do meet, and then depart.
But always their mysterious dart
Leaves one bleeding, just plain stifling,
Accounting for your suffering.
But realize this solemn truth
That when you see you lose a tooth
Always appears a better one
Equal in love to so far none.

So if you feel like deflating,
All down and out contemplating
That something good had passed you by,
Well, think again, my sweetie pie.
For hearts do meet and then depart
But soon your happiness will start.
And when you feel sorrow and pain,
Cheer up at your upcoming gain

Come Rain or Come Shine

And so it began that one day we met
I, lonely and shy, you, not woman yet.
In each other's eyes we looked for friendship
But love strong and bold was all that we reap.
Against the fierce storm and the vile canine
I said I'd love you come rain or come shine.

And so we set up for this our journey,
No weapons on board; you in jail, I free,
Not a common ground to debate our fears,
Not a common friend to offer a cheer.
We kept on true north, left the world behind
And still I love you come rain or come shine.

Then came the time of dreadful curse,
With low blows we did not rehearse.
We lost the treasure so cherished,
All sad and blue, weary, finished…

And so it became that upon the trees
The birds to their songs inflicted a freeze
And the mighty sun to Mother Nature
Never sent its rays, to her displeasure.
For the universe, since you were not mine,
Echoing my heart did not rain or shine.

And so in this life when you see the end
A new beginning is often at hand.
In each other's eyes we gaze for answers
But strong love echoed over and over.
Therefore I promised, with your hand in mine,
To love you always come rain or come shine.

Run my Letter

For an eternity
My heart has been lonely,
Finally it open'
To a jolly maiden.
It emerged suddenly from its hibernation
And is dying to love; carry its petition,
Run my letter, run.

Don't go on lingering,
Don't go mind your own thing.
You should get up and leave,
Ignore other missive'
Who occupy your time with their petty gossips
When they should deliver what is sealed with their lips,
Run my letter, run.

When she opens her eyes
Discerning your disguise,
Beg her to consider
The weight of my offer.
She'll read between your lines and detect at a glance
That my life without her will not stand any chance,
Run my letter, run.

Tell her I will always
Warm her nights, cheer her days.
Remind her that never
Will my feelings waver,
That my sun will always retire in her sea,
That I will always smile for her brown eyes to see.
Run my letter, run.

Amour Pour Amour

With blood and sweat and tears and sufferings alike,
Cross bearing, back tearing, crown wearing made of spikes,
See my child, in order to win over your love,
The complicated schemes planned by your God above.

You will never picture the dark alternative,
The dreadful curse His death has managed to reprieve.
Since your loving Father devised it all for you,
Your pledge of loyalty to Him you should renew.

For the life that you live, be it happy or sad,
Full of joy that gladdens or pain that gets you mad,
Will in return reveal the depth of gratitude
The Christian, to his God, displays with attitude.

First Christmas

On that eve, on that night,
Cold and dark to your sight,
You set out to find
A place to rest your mind.
You were thinking of such
A son who would be yours
And be God's just as much;
Laden with divine chores.

Mother, do you recall
The pain you did endure;
First from the baby's call
Then the inn displeasure?
You were young and so pure
It was hard to be sure
Of the promise God made
To use you as His maid.

But you had faith in Him,
Trusted His divine scheme.
So you replied: "I do"
To the Spirit in you.
But the fact did remain;
In your visceral girth
That you were cold, in pain;
Had no place to give birth.

So in a poor manger
You laid your divine Son
On that hay to shiver,
First cross to carry on.
You received the first gift
On that first Christmas day;
God's Love to you bequeathed
And to a world astray.

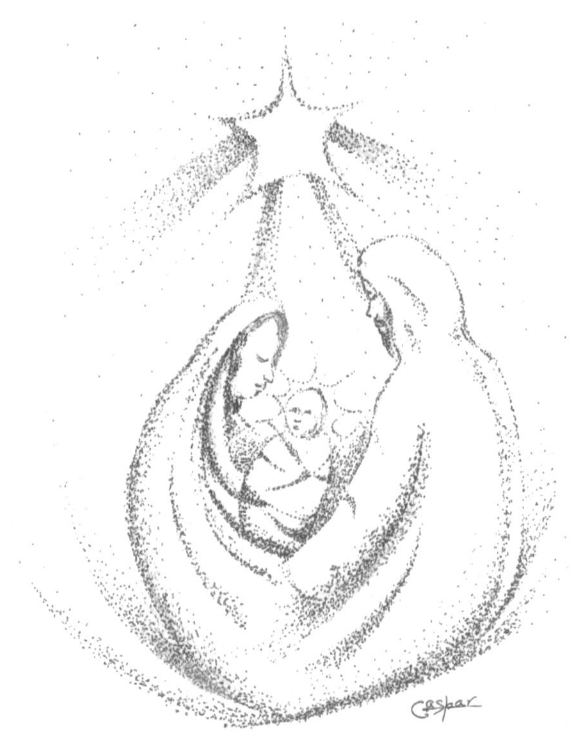

John and Di

We all must have been told,
Long before we grow old,
Of this world end nearing
And the Lord's wrath fearing.

Some of us changed their ways,
Invested for those days.
Others kept the samba
And the vida loca.

History will narrate
Days of terrible fate
When just before the blaze
They still ate, drank in daze.

We sat and watched in pain
The dive of that small plane,
And heard before from France
Crash the dear lady prince.

But still we overlook
To warn us, lives it took. . .
If not end of the world,
Think of end of your world.

To Giovanni

My child
Come and sit by me
It's wild
How you cannot see
How sweet
Is your infancy.
It's neat
Not have to worry,
Better
Not to feel the pain
Linger
Like a bad migraine
Over
Though you fight in vain.

See child,
Your sweet infancy
Is mild
And free of worry.
Don't try
To hurry the time,
Don't lie
You will lose your prime.
Hold on
To your innocence,
Bonbons
Are of the essence,
To play
Do pledge allegiance.

One day
If the Lord permits
Away
From your trick or treats
You'll say
The soul in the pits;
Why time
Has gone by so fast,
Its chime
Has been so steadfast
To add
Lines on your forehead
But sad
No wisdom instead.

Listen
Soon your time will come
Often
You will be lonesome.
Deepen
Your faith in your Lord
For then
Only you'll afford
The pain
Old age has in store
But now
You should just ignore
The how
And why love is for.

So lad
Return to your game
Be glad
You don't have to blame
Your glands
Or your pants in flame
Cause hence
You'd experience shame.
Today
Go hop and rejoice
And play
For it is God's choice.
Later
Will be here so soon
Better
Go play with the moon.

Criticism

There will be days of theme so sad
When talks of true color will clash.
These days when the good and the bad
Ring out in tunes of words made harsh.

And you'll be told of your weak points
For they annoy the meekest heart
And in return, blanking the point
You will disclose her fickle part.

Then in the spirit of exchange
You'll discover in her mirror
The you that you could rearrange
To appease her dormant furor

But all the while you'll discover
That though loving and well docile,
Your dear significant other
Is far from being an imbecile.

And you'll accept the harsh critics
As anchor of a brand new you,
Who with more actions than lyrics
The knots of traits, try to undo.

Don't fall apart if come what may
Tomorrow brings your appraisal
That reveals you are the same way
Though you thought got rid of it all.

See, human nature is just that;
The only way that one can be.
Unless the Maker of the pot
Decides to unfold His mercy.

There, only then you see the change
That usually people applaud.
For it's striking and even strange,
As night and day, deserving laud.

Be receptive of finger point,
Mostly the ones closer to you.
Overlooking could disappoint
The chances of a self brand new.

For there'll be days when themes are sad
When talks of traits may sound too harsh.
Often with honesty, my lad,
You'll rid yourself of heavy trash.

Simple Hint

We fight and we fight
To get what we deserve.
We fight but we might
Miss what's for us reserved.

We long and we long
For somebody to love
But ignore the strong
Signs given from above.

We pray and we pray
Our load to lessen
But in different ways
We wrong our brethren.

Let's long, fight and pray
To inherit our love
But please, mind the way
That the brethren we shove.

I Don't Love You

I don't love you cause you're beautiful,
I love you for you embellish my world.
I don't love you cause you're sensitive
I love you cause you give sense to my life.
I don't love you for the love you give,
I love you cause it makes me feel like flying.
I don't love you for your warm touch,
I love you for you never cease to embrace me.
I don't love you for your kisses,
I just stifle without the air you breathe.
I don't love you for your kind words
But they keep me going in all that I do.
I don't love you for the good times we have
But without you my time seems to stand still.
I don't love you cause you're my baby,
I love you for you are the only one I'll ever have.
I don't love you more when you are far away
But every day is a good day if it starts with the sound of your voice.
I don't want to give you the rest of my life
But rather I rest knowing I'm blessed to have you in my life.

T.G.I. Friday

The sun tired again sends off its weakest beams
Over the calm waters of the Harlem River.
A lively group of youths with military screams
In disorderly rows are running all over.

At these dragging moments of evening rush hours
A wave of motorists having Jersey in mind,
Racing to reach the G.W.B. towers,
Are beating each other in manners not so kind.

At this time of the year when nature finally
Releases in the air long expected degrees
And the heat all over hangs the haze lazily,
You can feel in the throats the hays of miseries.

It's N.Y. in the spring, one evening, early May.
The back up is so long that you wish you could walk.
All the faces you see say T.G.I. Friday,
H.R. Drive, Friday eve; it can last an epoch.

End of Day

At the end of my day, slowly I take my load
Of peaceful sentiments I gained from completion
Of the burdens the world that day chose to unload
And put on my shoulders with no hesitation.

At the end of my day though I feel much alert
I perceive already my spirit all willing
To take its nightly stroll and leave behind inert
My all-weary body from daily chores battling.

Though I know tomorrow I will start all over,
I trust the sun will shine again on my meadow.
For to hope is to live and to live is never
Lose sight of any dream, come joy or come sorrow.

At the end of my day therefore, I don't despair
Knowing day after day the sun shines on the dew.
The only balm that soothes my body wear and tear
Is to open my heart and think freely of you.

Excerpts

True strength is in essence
An unreachable dream
Unless one in advance
Of his flaws, hears the screams.

x

For on the path of life
There is good and evil;
This is the mother strife
Of the Alter Ego.

x

The burning desire
To upstream in her sea
Generates the fire
That in my frame you see.

x

Of your eyes the pure jade
Lights a bridge to your soul.
I don't know what I'd trade
To afford the stiff toll.

Into my life you came one day
Like the goldest of suns
But with you came the coldest day
That I have ever known…

x

Your broken heart had been stepped on
As were last autumn fallen leaves.
Before dawns another season
The will to love you will retrieve.

x

Come closer, I want to whisper
The love I feel for you.
The sun and moon will forever
Daily tell you its true.

x

If ever you want to cherish
The ones you hold so near,
Give them what will never perish;
The love you hold so dear.

In the indigo sky appears
The brilliance of two lonely stars;
No hug and kiss but lots of tears
For always they remain afar.

x

If one day on your window pane
Re-appears this lonely swallow,
Think of me who searches in vain
Of your bright eyes the lovely glow.

x

The cross we bear in older days
Is hammered in the youth.
We carry it in various ways
Cursing this golden truth.

x

Always hope for better days.
As the sun will shine
The Lord sends always our way
His mercy divine.

When of the mocking bird
The golden voice is heard,
Say, who can decipher
Its plea to the Creator?

X

Always the way you make your bed
You come and rest your weary head.
Be mindful of your daily deeds;
They are of your dreams the true seeds.

Très Jolie

You're lovely as a rose,
Oh but it sounds so cheap!
You're beautiful because
All flowers in a heap
Could not even come close
To your beauty so deep…

You see how pitiful
And borderline trivial
I become though thoughtful
And politely genial.
The words I want to say
Get scrambled in my mind,
You take my breath away,
Leave me dumb, leave me blind…

The early morning sea,
The golden rising sun
Forever seem to be
In perfect unison
To offer the heavens
And all the fading stars
The pure glow of your lens',
Your calm of surest pars.
You always inspire
The most peaceful feeling

For in this attire
I can perceive the string
Of angels who fire
Love in you, deep within
So that it transpires
For all the birds to sing.

For wherever you go
Love springs like a geyser,
All of us here below
Fall one and one after
Stunned by the lovely glow
Your joyful eyes offer…
But like a free sparrow
You don't ever hover.

Therefore in this sheer misery,
This life during which we suffer
Your light steadily will carry
My heart from where it did linger.
You touch my soul so lovingly
That deep inside I could favor
The peaceful and lovely Mary
When first touched by the Creator
To receive her Son most holy.

Rupture

And when we don't see eye to eye,
When we tango with truths and lies,
The promises of faithfulness
Lay much too heavy on the chests.

We examine all solutions,
Try to tone down the reactions
Of the grievance the counterpart
Imposes on our loving heart.

Often we make a point
Solely to kill a doubt
But when love's out of joint
The common sense runs out.

So when we don't se eye to eye
The least of affections will die
For in the midst of bitter tears
The voice of hate comes loud and clear.

We redirect our weary steps
From many fights ridded of pep,
With wounded heart and silent cries
For then we don't see eye to eye.

Serenity

The fading sunset glow of evening firmament
Puts a magical crown on the mountains dormant.
The night entertainers and insects all alike
Soar with their thrilling buzz, the eventide to spike.

And the silent waters reflecting golden dreams
With the blissful azure compete or so it seems,
Instilling in the hearts a touch of gentleness,
Heralding of the night the blessed quietness.

And the subtle shadows emerging from the ground
Lull with muttered kisses either vale, either mound.
The wind softly blowing awakes all the senses
To rustic aromas of far away fences.

See a lonely swallow rushing back to the nest
To warm up its young ones since the sun took its rest.
Nature in unison ever seems to mutter
Grateful and loving words toward the Creator.

The Frown

Alone in the dark I stay
Trying hard to find a way
That eventually would play
Right into this disarray.

My life with all its events;
Steep ups and scary descents,
Bring out of me great complaints.
Please folks, listen to my vents.

For long before I was born
Under this sign Capricorn
Life has been but a big thorn
Fit to kill any greenhorn.

If at times I frown at you,
Get cranky at who knows who,
May it be to someone new
Or a victim through and through,

I deeply hope you forgive
For one day I will retrieve
From this life the will to live
And to you folks my smile, give.

For as long as I perform
Acting out of the norm,
What come to me will take form
Of the kindness I deform.

For as Mother Earth is round
The bad vibe you send around
Will seek you till you are found
And to you bring the same frown.

Please, Stand Watch with me

You will carry burdens on your weary shoulders,
Will despair, will falter and often will lose hope.
You will in your sorrow relentlessly ponder
Why is the road so long and whether to elope.

Painfully you'll notice this devastating truth
That from your same brethren you will suffer plenty
But in this dark garden where you pray for a truce
Will you too, will you not, please stand a watch with Me?

All the promises made to the ones before you
Are reiterated into you yearning soul.
Don't let the glittering of your time dim your view
Lest you lose your true north and yourself as a whole.

At great many a costs, the path you should follow
Has been set before you to ward off infamy.
At even greater price, through pain and through sorrow
More than ever before you should stand watch with Me?

But soon one blessed day, in any near future,
After this night of watch, when your sun will come shine,
Revealing to the world how precious and nurtured
Are the ones, who treasure the gift of Love divine,

After the night is through, after tears, after mourn,
When the dawn comes shining in the eyes of many,
You will stand jubilant in the light of that morn
Knowing that through it all you stood a watch with Me.

Two Brides

For in this world
There are two brides
Only.
One full of pride
And one who lives
Humbly.
Don't ever think
That might remains
Solely
Into the hands
Of the strong and
Pretty.
For in this world
There are two brides
Only.
Hurry decide
Which one you will
Marry.

Nature's Song

It has been a long time,
Life can be such a drag.
It has been a long time
Seen with my rhyme I bragged.

Many times the sunrise
Offered to my sad eyes
The warmth of its promise
But its wonder I missed.

And the moon secretly
Stroke my cheek peacefully
Telling my weary soul
Of my dreams to keep hold.

And the relentless sea
Sang lovely tunes to me
Where love, success and chance
Rhyme with blessed patience.

So the birds in the air
Eager to make it fair
Echoed this melody,
Witnessing God's mercy.

For Nature in essence
Attest the Providence
And brings to us daily
Hope for this long journey.

It has been a long time…
Though one can be so bored
Let me fashion my rhyme
To Nature's loving chords.

You're on my Mind

What a blissful delight to have you on my mind,
Painfully realize how much I miss you blind.
It comes to me always when I expect the least
And my poor heart bleeding gets me to clench my fist.

A loving heart remains a gift from God above.
Despite our failings He still shows us His love.
But in love we often fail to grasp one detail;
Of a coin love's the head and suffering the tail.

So love my lonely heart and then bleed thereafter,
Slowly you will favor the One of your Master.
For He loves steadily with nothing in return;
For your remote angel you have to bleed and yearn.

So I say I love you, my far away angel,
You who brighten my day and my dark night dispel.
For the blissful feeling to have you on my mind,
Though it lightens my load, makes that I miss you blind.

Perseverance

For all the painful hours
You suffered for my sake
I'll unveil My power
For your eyes to partake.

You remained there steady
When your sun did not shine,
Even when all weary
You kept your hand in Mine.

I watched you tread and fall,
Sighed when your poor heart bled,
And when you gave up all
Sorrowful tears I shed.

But in My love for you
I kept you on the road;
It was hard, full of grue,
So I carried your load.

Then Mine you will remain
Until the end of time
And you'll prove loud and plain
How love and suff'ring rhyme.

Ecce Homo

This is My Son, this is My Son,
The One on whom My favor rests.
This is my Son, through Him alone
My people find My very best.

This is My Son, this is My Son
Sent to redeem My people sins,
Yearned for and promised for so long,
With divine treasures indwelling.

This is My Son, this is My Son
Ever willing to die for you,
The chosen Lamb, the holy One,
Voucher of a covenant new.

Sightlessness

Blindness is not at all by a leash being led
By one of man's best friend, walking with steps of lead,
Aimlessly turning head following a vague stare,
Behind set of dark shades, seemingly grasping air.
It is not just missing the changing tones of sky
And steady formation of birds migrating by.
Nor is it to perceive the warmth of the sunrays
Yet missing the nuances provoked by their arrays.
It's not feeling the cold on a winter morning
But still miss icicles on tree branches hanging.

Blindness is the cold fate of those who can perceive
At the end of the day the sea the sun, retrieve.
Watch moon appearances the time of month, dictate
And the stars the coming of the seasons, relate.
Experiencing Nature bewildering beauty
And not feel deep within love springing suddenly.
Measure all the oceans, sizing their many shores,
Considering the sun, ponder its many chores
Yet in coldness remain unwilling to admit
That all was created by God's Loving Spirit.

A Song

Give me a song
And I'll give you my soul,
Sing it along
And slowly take control
Of the bondless beauty
That lies within every
Creature upon the earth.

Give me a song
And I'll give you my heart
Echoing strong
With rhymes that set apart
The many, many dreams
Of peaceful, loving themes
That from your eyes take birth.

Give me a song
I'll eclipse misery.
It won't be long
Before sheer harmony
Comes set upon your world
And brings you the rare pearl
Of peace within your girth.

For with a song
You shuffle the seasons
And on and on,
Restore the impressions
Of the soul younger days
Made of stars in arrays
And love with a nipple
Straight from Heaven's bottle.

Midnight

(The night)

And the keyboard morose
Resounds the artist's song.
It's always one of those
Speaking of love so strong.

And the smokes permeate
All corners of the room.
You don't need any date,
Just your drink and your gloom.

For the notes in the air
Recall the past affairs.
Since we are no more pair,
The reveries are all Claire's.

But soon after day breaks
You'll face again the plight,
That old truth that still aches…
But now enjoy the night.

First Date

You looked so beautiful tonight,
You came prepared to set things right.
And the funniest thing of all
Is that you never heard the call
My lonely soul sent out to you,
Unknown angel to my rescue.

You looked so beautiful tonight.
Got to admit, I felt His might.
It's been so long I felt like this,
Hoped so much that it'd be a bliss…
But if instead we don't connect…
Well, then you'll miss the sad effect.

You looked so beautiful tonight
Even the stars and moon were bright
Though in the air we felt the bliss.
You looked pretty, I must insist.
But just in case from your viewpoint
My past, your eyes, would disappoint,
My heart will keep the memory
Of how tonight you looked lovely.

Immaculate Conception Feast

And they all came and sang,
It was a lovely day.
Not feasted with a bang,
Only to sing and pray.

It seemed, that in her grace
The blessed Queen of cores,
On everybody's face,
Had impressed her Son's score.

So we sang and we prayed
And the Spirit filled us.
We felt His Might displayed,
Subtle yet vigorous.

Pearly gate of Heaven,
So spotlessly conceived,
Accept our refrains
And prayers please, receive.

Within our bosom
Please give birth to your Son.
Make that His kingdom come
In hearts of everyone.

Ave Maris Stella,
Mater piissima,
Mater purissima,
Mater sanctissima.

Through Centuries

From yesterday
To nowadays
Around the sun
The Earth has spun.

From yesterday
To nowadays
When comes the spring
All the birds sing.

Nothing on earth comes from nothing.
Whatsoever that nature brings
That repeatedly marvels us
To the elders has been precious.
It may be fair, it may be not,
But nothing new on earth is brought.

From yesterday
To nowadays
Blue sky above
Inspire love.

From yesterday
To nowadays
True loving hearts
Will mend their parts.

True Love

Love blinds the jolly heart;
Brought by old Cupid's dart,
Intoxicating the senses,
Tearing down the inner fences
Built over experience
Of all the tangos danced.

Love tames the fickle heart,
Snuggling its every part,
With themes of blue sky in April,
With hopes as when we were little.
Therefore the heart in trance
Forgives any offence.

Love soothes the bleeding heart
In ways much more too smart
For us the knowledge to fathom
And store in our safe bottom.
It's given in a glance
By Divine Providence.

Wise Thoughts

I wish one day to let you know
How much I miss your lovely face
And hunger for your warm embrace

And then in turn hear the echo
Of your heart whispering to me
Words of angelic melody.

For senselessly we hold inside
Confessions of a bleeding heart,
Impulses felt right from the start.

Often the words stifled with pride
Remained sealed in our bosom
When with no clue our time comes.

I Wish You

Before you go, before you go
Let me to your thoughts give echo.
And now that our roads break apart
Let us hope for a brand new start.

I wish you shadow in the sun,
In your sorrow, some kind of fun.
When all seem empty and just cold,
I wish you a warm hand to hold.

I wish you flowers in your spring,
The kind you see when your heart sings,
Rich in color, in shape and form,
Which your sadness to joy, transform.

I wish you rain on your meadow,
Insight into your tomorrow.
Learn not to ever, ever fear
And from your weakness when to steer.

I wish you peace within your midst.
Of your neighbors respect the least.
Always offer kind utterance
Even in face of connivance.

I wish you health in your bosom,
Steady gait when the old days come.
And since the heart is so fickle
I wish you friends in your circle

For love, see, is like a sparrow,
Takes flight before it's tomorrow
And with a subtle, skillful art,
Departs after stealing your heart.

Kingdom of Love

Within the realm of our love,
This feeling sent from God above,
Within the circle of our love
Your stamp remains strong and steady.

Within the kingdom of my love,
This rush I can't get enough of,
On the empire of my love
You reign as queen with majesty.

And I the servant, the subject,
Leavened by this awesome effect,
My bleeding heart you will protect
From its impending misery.

For the blessed, treasured feeling
We use as if it were a fling
To obtain the forbidden thing
Will always find us unworthy.

That same Spirit who delivers,
The Advocate, the Comforter
Will not dwell in us if ever
We don't keep His word faithfully…

The love you bring I will treasure,
Will love you beyond all measure,
You, source of my divine pleasure,
Who took over my heart swiftly.

For the kingdom of our love,
This most blessed thing from above,
This rush I can't get enough of,
You rule over, my sweet Erie.

Child of Mine

There's a peaceful feeling,
Warm as the end of spring
That surges from my heart,
Gains everybody part.

It caresses my soul
And slowly takes control
Of my heart's sturdy pace
To make over my face.

It entertains my mind,
Shuts the whole world behind,
Leaves me in ecstasy
With your face, my chérie.

It gives me strength I need
And my libido feeds,
Takes me for a joy ride.
The reaction I hide.

So if you see the trace
Of a smile on my face
It's because the Divine
By His grace, made you mine.

Happy B'day

The sun shined its most golden rays
And the daffodils sprang anew.
The glitter from the morning dew
Reflected glows of festive days.

The jovial sparrow tuned its cords
And stretched its wings for a first flight.
A string of hay ran out of sight
At the speed the brook could afford.

The rooster with uncanny clout,
That the flowers seem to echo,
Re-encores its pompous solo
To the Heavens as happy shout.

And so Mother Nature displays
The lovely mood imposed on her…
What's the occasion, you wonder,
But, my dear, it is your birthday!

Gethsemane

He loved His Father to that very extent
That in the garden on His knees to lament
He begged for His life, "Please, Father find a way,
Have pity on Me, save Me Father, I pray."

Seeing His anguish, the dreadful curse facing
God sent His angel, divine strength to Him bring.
After He gave up His body to consume
God gave Him glory but not at all posthumed…

I love You my Lord to that very extent
That with my burden at Your feet I lament.
I beg for Your help, "Please my Lord, find a way,
Have pity on me, save me Master, I pray

Seeing my anguish, the heavy load bearing,
Jesus, Your Spirit, consolations will bring.
And as you promise, if myself I inhume,
Your divine treasures to me you will exhume.

Believe in Your God for the trust you put in,
With the same graces He will fill you within.
The very meters that you measure your God
Are the dimensions of blessings you'll afford.